Claire Masurel

# No, No, Titus!

Illustrated by Shari Halpern

**HOUGHTON MIFFLIN**   BOSTON • MORRIS PLAINS, NJ

California   •   Colorado   •   Georgia   •   Illinois   •   New Jersey   •   Texas

*For Pierson Broadwater—C.M.*
*For Bernadette and Matt—S.H.*

NO, NO, TITUS! by Claire Masurel, illustrated by Shari Halpern. Text copyright ©
1997 by Claire Masurel. Reprinted by permission of North-South Books, Inc.

Houghton Mifflin Edition, 2005
Copyright © 2001 by Houghton Mifflin Company. All rights reserved.

Printed in the U.S.A.

ISBN 0-618-06702-7
9-B-05

"Welcome to your new home, Titus," said the farmer. "This farm needs a good dog!"

5

Titus wagged his tail. He wanted
to be a good dog. But what was a
good dog supposed to do?
The farm was big and everyone
was busy.

The school bus came down the road.

"HONK, HONK," went the school bus.

"WOOF, WOOF," barked Titus.

"No, no," said the children.

"Dogs don't go to school!"

The farmer was plowing the fields.

"VROOM, VROOM," went the tractor.

"WOOF, WOOF," barked Titus.

"No, no," said the farmer.

"Dogs don't drive tractors!"

The farmer's wife was milking.
"MOO, MOO," went the cow.
"WOOF, WOOF," barked Titus.
"No, no," said the cow.
"Dogs don't give milk!"

The farmer was plowing the fields.

"VROOM, VROOM," went the tractor.

"WOOF, WOOF," barked Titus.

"No, no," said the farmer.

"Dogs don't drive tractors!"

The farmer's wife was milking.

"MOO, MOO," went the cow.

"WOOF, WOOF," barked Titus.

"No, no," said the cow.

"Dogs don't give milk!"

The cat was chasing mice.
"MEOW, MEOW," went the cat.
"WOOF, WOOF," barked Titus.
"No, no," said the cat.
"Dogs don't chase mice."

The chickens were laying eggs.

"CLUCK, CLUCK," went the chickens.

"WOOF, WOOF," barked Titus.

"No, no," said the chickens.

"Dogs don't lay eggs."

Titus wanted to be a good farm dog.
But if dogs don't go to school,
or drive tractors, or give milk,
or catch mice, or lay eggs . . .
*what* was Titus supposed to do?
He crawled into his doghouse
and went to sleep.

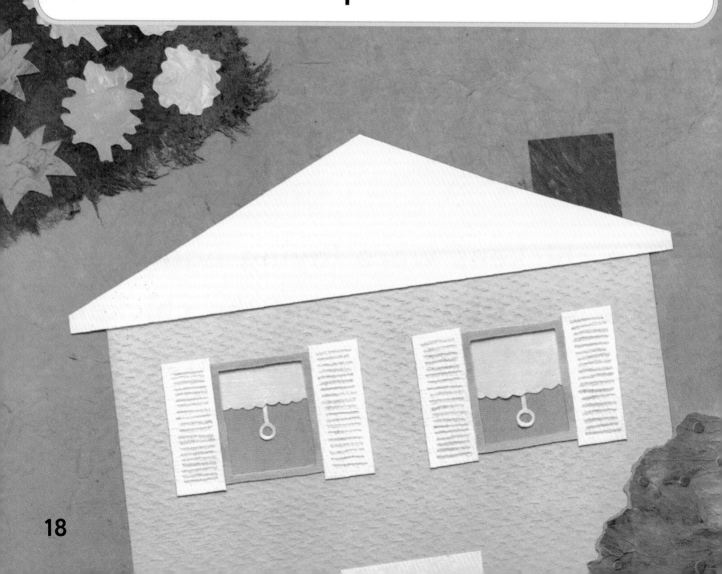

*Pitter, patter, pitter, patter.*
Something was going
to the chicken coop!
"WOOF, WOOF!" barked Titus.

The farmer came running.

"OH, NO!" shouted the farmer.

"A FOX!"

"WOOF! WOOF! WOOF!" barked Titus as he chased the fox across the field.

"YIP, YIP, YIP, YIP, YIP," cried the fox, and it disappeared into the forest.

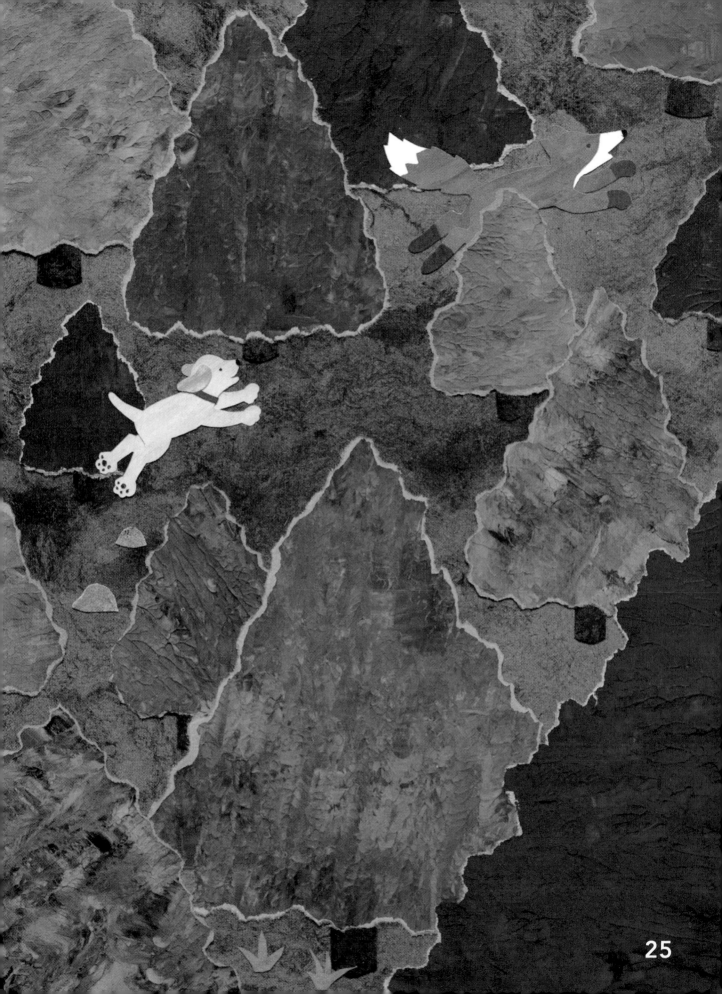

"HOORAY! HOORAY!" cheered the farmer, his wife, the children, and all the animals.

"What a good watchdog!"

"WOOF, WOOF!" barked Titus.

"WOOF! WOOF! WOOF!"